GREEK MYTHOLOGY

HERA,

Queen of the Gods

BY JOANNA BLAIR

Enslow PUBLISHING

Please visit our website, www.enslow.com. For a free color catalog of all our high-quality books, call toll free 1-800-398-2504 or fax 1-877-980-4454.

Cataloging-in-Publication Data
Names: Blair, Joanna.
Title: Hera, queen of the gods / Joanna Blair.
Description: Buffalo, NY : Enslow Publishing, 2027. | Series: Greek mythology | Includes glossary and index.
Identifiers: ISBN 9781978550926 (pbk.) | ISBN 9781978550933 (library bound) | ISBN 9781978550940 (ebook)
Subjects: LCSH: Hera (Greek deity)--Juvenile literature. | Goddesses, Greek--Juvenile literature. | Mythology, Greek--Juvenile literature.
Classification: LCC BL820.J6 B535 2027 | DDC 292.2114--dc23

Published in 2027 by
Enslow Publishing
2544 Clinton Street
Buffalo, NY 14224

Portions of this work were originally authored by Christine Ha and published as *Hera*. All new material in this edition was authored by Joanna Blair.

Cover Designer: Joshua Olson
Interior Designer: Joshua Olson
Editor: Claire Vanden Branden

Photo Credits: Cover, pp. 1, 6–7, 29 IMG Stock Studio/Shutterstock.com; pp. 4–5 Lev Paraskevopoulos/Shutterstock.com; pp. 8–9 Gilmanshin/Shutterstock.com; pp. 10–11 van der Haven/Shutterstock.com; pp. 12–13 Konstantin Zozulya/Shutterstock.com; p. 13 Pandrea World/Shutterstock.com; pp. 14–15 Vivienne Morel/Shutterstock.com; pp. 16–17 kapetsh/Shutterstock.com; pp. 18–19 Malchev/Shutterstock.com; pp. 20–21 Saima Photographer/Shutterstock.com; pp. 22–23 nbnserge/Shutterstock.com; pp. 24–25 Philip Birtwistle/Shutterstock.com; p. 26 mangojuicy/Shutterstock.com; p. 27 Jekatarinka/Shutterstock.com.

Printed in China

CPSIA compliance information: Batch #QS27ENS: For further information contact Enslow Publishing, at 1-800-398-2504.

TABLE OF CONTENTS

CHAPTER 1

THE QUEEN

Hera was the queen of the Greek gods. She was also the goddess of marriage and family. She was married to Zeus.

Hera and Zeus ruled over Mount Olympus in Greece.

Hera was powerful and smart. But she was also **vain**. She could be jealous and **vengeful**.

Hera often wore a crown. Sometimes, she carried a scepter.

In one story, Hera fought other goddesses over a golden apple.

Hephaestus was the god of fire and metalworking.

For example, one woman claimed she was as beautiful as Hera. Hera turned her into a stork.

FAMILY DRAMA

Hera did not get along with her son Hephaestus. She threw him off Mount Olympus. To get back at her, he made a beautiful throne. It trapped Hera when she sat on it.

Hera's sacred animals were the peacock and the cow. They often appear with her in art.

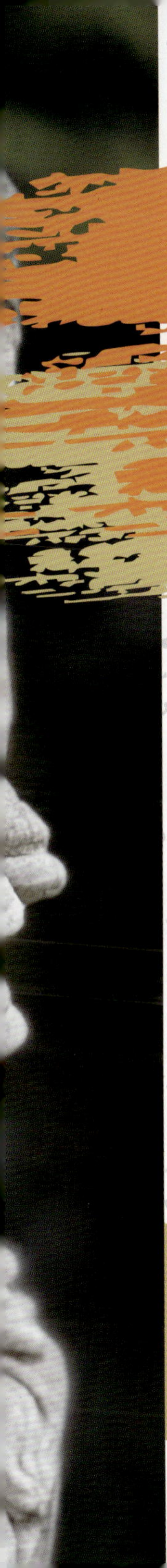

CHAPTER 2

HERA IN MYTHS

Hera had many powers. She could change shape. She could make people or animals do things. And she could control clouds and storms.

Hera often used her powers to get back at people who hurt her.

Nymphs are connected to parts of nature, such as mountains and rivers.

In one story, Hera was searching for Zeus. A **nymph** named Echo got in the way. So, Hera punished Echo. Echo could no longer talk on her own. She could only repeat what others said.

Greek gods sometimes came to Earth in disguise. Zeus became an animal. Hera turned into an old woman.

In one story, Zeus turned into a swan.

Zeus was king of the Greek gods.

Hera and Zeus had a big wedding. Another goddess gave Hera a wedding present. It was an enchanted tree. It produced beautiful golden apples.

HERA'S CHILDREN

Hera and Zeus had several children. One was Ares, the god of war. Hebe was another. She was the goddess of youth.

CHAPTER 3

UNHAPPY MARRIAGE

Zeus was not a faithful husband. He had many lovers. Hera disliked them and their children. She often tried to hurt them.

Hercules was the son of Zeus and a human. Hera tried to have monsters kill him.

In one story, Zeus fell in love with Io. Zeus turned Io into a cow to hide her from Hera. But his trick didn't work. Hera found the cow. She sent a giant to guard it.

Hera sometimes sent snakes or dragons to attack people she disliked.

Hera sent the giant Argus to keep Zeus away from Io. Argus had eyes all over his body.

After the giant Argus died, Hera moved his eyes to the tail of a peacock.

Zeus sent the god Hermes to kill the giant. In response, Hera sent a fly. It chased Io away.

A FIERY TRICK

Once, Zeus loved a human named Semele. Hera tricked them. She got Zeus to show Semele his true form. Seeing it made Semele burst into flames.

CHAPTER 4

WORSHIPPING HERA

Many Greek women prayed to Hera. Some prayed about their families or marriages. Others asked for help having babies.

In Rome, Hera was known as Juno. She was said to guard the whole Roman Empire.

Across Greece, festivals were held to honor Hera. One took place in Olympia. It was a sports festival for female athletes. Girls ran races.

The Temple of Hera in Olympia is one of the oldest temples in Greece.

SPORTS IN GREECE

Olympia held a sports festival for Zeus, too. It was called the Olympics. For a while, only men could **compete**. But women sometimes owned the horses or **chariots** they used.

Hera was also the **guardian** of two cities. Their names were Argos and Samos. Hera protected them.

Ruins of Hera's temple still stand in Samos today.

Pomegranate trees have grown in Greece since ancient times.

Hera is sometimes shown holding a pomegranate. In ancient Greece, this fruit was a **symbol** of **fertility**.

TEST YOUR KNOWLEDGE

Take this quiz to test your knowledge.

1. Write a few sentences explaining the main ideas of Chapter 2.
2. Do you think it was fair for Hera to attack Zeus's children? Why or why not?
3. Which animal was sacred to Hera?
   - A. the fly
   - B. the peacock
   - C. the stork
4. Why would Zeus not want Hera to find Io?
   - A. Io would make Hera go away.
   - B. Io would like Hera more than him.
   - C. Hera would probably try to hurt Io.

5. What does **faithful** mean in this book?

*Zeus was not a **faithful** husband. He had many lovers.*

- **A.** staying true to one person or idea
- **B.** being hard to trust or rely on
- **C.** being a bad example to others

6. What does **athletes** mean in this book?

*It was a sports festival for female **athletes**. Girls ran races.*

- **A.** people who start a fire
- **B.** people who rule a country
- **C.** people who do a sport

Answers can be found on page 32.

GLOSSARY

chariots
Two-wheeled carts pulled by horses or other animals.

compete
To try to beat others in a game or event.

fertility
The ability to have babies.

guardian
A person who protects something or someone.

nymph
A beautiful spirit that lives in trees, water, or other parts of nature.

sacred
Having close ties to a god, goddess, or religion.

scepter
A staff held by a ruler as a symbol of power.

symbol
An object or idea that stands for and reminds people of something else.

vain
Caring a lot about how you look.

vengeful
Wanting to hurt someone who has hurt you.

FOR MORE INFORMATION

BOOKS

Krekelberg, Alyssa. *Greek Myths and Legends.* Minneapolis, MN: Jump!, Inc., 2026.

Lock, Deborah. *Greek Myths.* New York, NY: DK Publishing, 2023.

WEBSITES

Britannica Kids: Hera
kids.britannica.com/kids/article/Hera/353240
Read more myths about Hera.

National Geographic Kids: The Gods and Goddesses of Ancient Greece!
natgeokids.com/nz/discover/history/greece/greek-gods
Learn more about Greek gods and goddesses.

Publisher's note to educators and parents: Our editors have carefully reviewed these websites to ensure that they are suitable for students. Many websites change frequently, however, and we cannot guarantee that a site's future contents will continue to meet our high standards of quality and educational value. Be advised that students should be closely supervised whenever they access the internet.

INDEX

Answer Key:
1. Answers will vary; 2. Answers will vary; 3. B; 4. C; 5. A; 6. C